THE FIREBIRD

JANE YOLEN

ILLUSTRATED BY

VLADIMIR VAGIN

HARPERCOLLINSPUBLISHERS

The Firebird
Text copyright © 2002 by Jane Yolen
Illustrations copyright © 2002 by Vladimir Vagin
Printed in Hong Kong. All rights reserved.
www.harperchildrens.com

Library of Congress Cataloging-in-Publication Data
Yolen, Jane.
Firebird, The / by Jane Yolen ; illustrated by Vladimir Vagin.
p.   cm.
Summary: A retelling of the Russian folktale in which Prince Ivan encounters
the magical Firebird who helps him defeat the evil Kostchei.
ISBN 0-06-028538-9. — ISBN 0-06-028539-7 (lib. bdg.)
[1. Fairy tales. 2. Folklore—Russia.]   I. Vagin, Vladimir Vasilévich, date, ill.
II. Zhar-ptitsa. English.   III. Title.
PZ8.Y78Fi   2002
398.2'0947'02—dc21   99-36811
[E]   CIP
                                                                            AC

Typography by Al Cetta
1 2 3 4 5 6 7 8 9 10
❖
First Edition

For Maria Tallchief, first and greatest of the Firebirds

—J.Y.

To my dear friend Drasko Kovrlija and to his family

—V.V.

In a certain land, in a certain kingdom—as they say in old Russia—on the far side of a certain tangled wood, a garden shimmered like a green jewel. The garden belonged to the wizard Kostchei the Deathless—so called, it was said, because he could not be killed.

A golden fence surrounded the garden. Paths wound about the tall garden trees. Stone statues that were once living men stared with stone eyes at the captive princess and her nine maidens, the only beings alive in Kostchei's garden.

All this the red bird saw as it flew down on wings of flame.
Firebird!

Firebird had come to steal the golden fruits growing in
Kostchei's garden—the magical fruits that made its voice so clear.
How clear? You could hear it every day for a week and not tire of it.
That clear.

There was only one other living thing in the tangled wood.

Prince Ivan.

He had been lost for three days and three nights seeking the brutish boar, the shadowy elk, the fleet deer. He had searched the stream for fish to catch with his bare hands.

But he had found nothing, for in Kostchei's forest nothing lived.

Tired, hungry, full of despair, Prince Ivan sank down on his knees among the ferns and prayed. As he prayed, the bright-red bird flashed past.

His quick hands caught the bird, imprisoning it.

The bird fluttered. It struggled. It flung itself against Prince Ivan's hands, but it could not escape.

So it spoke to the prince in a voice of fire.

Oh, Prince of Russia, set me free.
A magic gift I will give thee.

Did he accept?

This was magic. Any prince would have been a fool not to accept.

Prince Ivan was certainly no fool. He opened the bars of his fingers and the bird flew free, leaving only a feather bright as a flame behind.

Prince Ivan tucked the feather inside his shirt, where it felt warm over his heart.

As Firebird flew off, it called back:

Wave the feather in the air—
Firebird will be right there.

Prince Ivan could have just let Firebird fly away.
But he was a hunter. And he was no fool. Running swiftly,
he followed the bird through the forest to the forest's edge, over a
meadow, past a stream, up a hill, down again, coming at last to a great
golden fence.

"Where there is a fence, there will be a house," Prince Ivan told
himself. "And where there is a house, there will be food."

He was very hungry.

How right he was! On the other side of the fence was a house.
Prince Ivan knocked on the door, and ten beautiful maidens
let him in. They were alike as sisters, but the one with the darkest hair
and the reddest lips and the boldest manner stepped forward.

"Go from here," she said. "You are in great danger if you stay.
Our master is Kostchei the Deathless, the wizard of darkness.
He turns to stone anyone who tries to rescue us. Only we are alive
in all his realm."

She pointed to the garden and the stone statues.
Prince Ivan grew cold at her words. Only the feather over
his heart remained warm.
"I am not afraid," he said, though he was.

"If you would free us," the princess told him, "then you must fight Kostchei's demons in the garden. If by luck you manage to defeat them, you will still have to kill The Deathless."

Prince Ivan trembled. How could he kill him who could not die?

The princess continued, "Do not look Kostchei in the eye. Do not say his name. He has power over you only if you let him." She smiled at Prince Ivan, and her smile gave him strength. She kissed him, and her kiss lent him warmth.

"I will try," said Prince Ivan. He turned and went out into the garden to await the demons.

He did not have to wait long.

In the garden, demons sidled through the slits of the great golden fence. They had horns and tails, long teeth and forked tongues. They had cruel yellow nails and curious yellow eyes.

With great snarls and growls they fell upon Prince Ivan and, despite his heroic struggles, forced him to the ground. Their large hands curled around his throat and closed.

As he began to lose consciousness, Prince Ivan remembered the princess and her kiss. He remembered how it had warmed him.

Warm.

There was something warm—even glowing—under his shirt. It was not the remembered kiss keeping him warm. It was Firebird's feather!

Now he really remembered. Freeing an arm, he reached into his shirt and pulled out the feather, bright as flame.

The demons' hands dropped from Prince Ivan's throat. The horned ones fell back, afraid of the feather's magic. Prince Ivan leaped to his feet.

Using the feather like a whip, he chased the monsters, driving them from one side of the garden to the other. Some dropped to the ground, exhausted.

But after a few minutes the feather began to lose its heat.

Sensing that the feather's power had been used up, the demons began to advance again.

"Firebird!" Prince Ivan called as he waved the feather in the air. "I need you."

At once the air around Prince Ivan grew hazy and hot, shimmering like a summer's day.

On wings of flame Firebird flew into the garden, a magic golden sword clutched in its talons.

Seeing this, the demons began to wail for their master, Kostchei, for they knew that only he could save them now.

At the demons' calls Kostchei appeared in a dark cloud. He had long black hair and a black mustache, drooping like the wings of a dying raven. His fingernails were as long as his hands. A crown of golden spikes sat on his head.

"Look at me, Prince!" cried the wizard in a powerful voice. "Look into my eyes! My name is Kostchei. I am called The Deathless."

Prince Ivan trembled, but he did not look into the wizard's
eyes. He did not say the wizard's name. Once again he was
terribly cold.

But Firebird flew to the prince and dropped the golden sword
into his hands.

Taking the sword, Prince Ivan felt his courage return. He spun
about once to give himself momentum and plunged the magic sword
deep into Kostchei's chest.

And Kostchei the Deathless met Death at last.

Of course the statues turned back into handsome young men. Of course they took the hands of the nine maidens. Of course the tenth maiden—the princess with the darkest hair and the reddest lips and the boldest manner—and Prince Ivan were married.

And Firebird—well, Firebird flew away, never to be seen again. After all, the monsters had been routed, the wizard slain. What more was there to do but to dance?

As they used to say in old Russia—there's a tale for you, and a crock of butter for me.

A NOTE FROM THE AUTHOR

"Firebird," the story, and *Firebird*, the ballet, both come from Russian sources.

Kostchei the Deathless (also spelled Koschei or Koshchey) is a character about whom there are numerous folktales. As one critic has written, "The story of the immortal Kostchei is one of very frequent occurrence." Kostchei is always the villain of the story. Sometimes he is a snake; sometimes he lives in a cauldron, amid flames and boiling in pitch.

Firebird—also known as Zhar-Ptitsa—is also in many Russian tales. ("Zhar" is the Russian word that means heat, and "Ptitsa" is the word for bird, though not a particular kind.) In some stories Firebird dwells in a golden cage. Or feeds upon golden apples that have the power to bestow youth. Or—as in a Bohemian version—Firebird's song can heal the sick and restore sight to the blind.

Prince Ivan is a typical hero of Russian folktales—a good hunter, a lover of beautiful women, and handsome. Or, as the composer Igor Stravinsky has said, "simple, naïve, sometimes even stupid, devoid of all malice and . . . always victorious over characters that are clever, artful, complex, cruel, and powerful."

I first came upon the story of Firebird in the ballet, when Maria Tallchief as Firebird and Francisco Moncion as Prince Ivan performed in New York City on November 27, 1949. The ballet was choreographed for New York City Ballet by George Balanchine to music by Stravinsky.

I was one of the thousands of little girls who wanted to become ballerinas, but I was luckier than most. I got to train at Balanchine's School of American Ballet. We students were allowed to watch rehearsals, but only if we were absolutely quiet and did not move out of the room the entire time—not even to get something to eat or to go to the bathroom. Once out, you were not allowed back in!

One day Maria Tallchief hung her practice tutu on my locker. I took it as a sign. I vowed that I, too, would one day dance *Firebird*.

When I grew up, I no longer danced *en pointe*. In fact I no longer dance at all. But I feel that in this book I have kept my vow.

This book version is based on my memory of that classical ballet, with the help of *101 Stories of the Great Ballets* by George Balanchine and Francis Mason (New York: Anchor Books/Doubleday, 1989) as well as input from *Russian Folk-Tales* by William Ralston Shedden Ralston (New York: Arno Press, 1977), *The Three Kingdoms: Russian Folk Tales from Alexander Afanasiev's Collection*, illustrated by A. Kurkin (Moscow: Raduga Publishers, 1985), *The Fire-Bird: Russian Fairy Tales*, drawings by Igor Yershov and Ksenia Yershova (Moscow: Raduga Publishers, 1973), *Old Peter's Russian Tales* by Arthur Ransome (New York: Puffin Books, 1974; reprint of 1916 Nelson edition), *Myths and Folk-Tales of the Russians, Western Slavs, and Magyars* by Jeremiah Curtin (Boston: Little Brown and Company, 1890), and the classic *Russian Fairy Tales* by Aleksandr Afanas'ev, translated by Norbert Guterman (New York: Pantheon Books, 1945, 1973).